FOOL IN A BLUE HOUSE

Fool in a Blue House

POEMS

Katherine Gaffney

Manufactured in the United States of America
Printed on acid-free paper ∞
First Edition

On the Cover: Mary Cassatt, *Woman Bathing,* 1890-1891, color drypoint and aquatint on laid paper, 43.2 x 29.8 cm. Chester Dale Collection. Courtesy of National Gallery of Art, Washington, DC.

Cover design by Madeline Eisele

The University of Tampa Press
401 West Kennedy Boulevard
Tampa, FL 33606

ISBN(pbk.) 978-1-59732-198-3
ISBN (hbk.) 978-1-59732-197-6
ISBN (ebk.) 978-1-59732-199-0

Library of Congress Control Number: 2023935200

Browse & order online at
http://www.utampapress.org

For KS

Table of Contents

IV

V

Fool in a Blue House

let hair, nail cuttings
nourish the vine and fig tree

let man, woman
eat, be sheltered
—Adrienne Rich, "Tactile Value"

The Horse

This horse was born from a carousel; she tore off one morning when the man,
the one who took the tickets, smoked a cigarette and nursed a plastic cup
of coffee. Rain saturated her freedom—this birth is anything but. No mother
to lick the baby clean. No knock-kneed moments as baby works to balance.
She tore from the rods that held her in updown motion, kicked her rump high
and back, then rocked back on hind legs to punch the air: her eyes begging
for battle. How she found me is a story for another time, but I can say her head
was always near mine—resistance to law, docility, but how to say she honors.
How to tell you she teaches me to hold on, to bear what is her greatest kindness.
How her sunless birth helped me break, what it meant to feel the façade of control,
and then to gain it, for a moment. *Let me feel*, echoed by the roar of her hightail,
she taunts. With love to get on, to learn her body, mine.

I.

I would not think to touch the sky with two arms.

—Sappho

Like a Salmon (or Fool in a Blue House)

I feel like a fool in a blue house, thought I could curate
the life we'd live—repot herbs in spring, summer dinners
on the deck, year-round sex on the couch. Saturday
we'd bake bread. Sunday we'd walk in the sleepy
evening steadying ourselves for the week. But we've got
none of that, except for sex on the couch. He's bought
in, even with the front door open, weather permitting,
where extra quiet becomes a game we play. He says
his grandmother, in old age, was like a salmon,
wanting to return to Czechoslovakia, fuck, then die.
Fuck, then die, is a thought I've had in our bed—
how a woman in a too-large oxford shirt communicates
sex, for me, translates to never getting off
my my-size shirt. Please excuse the post-it notes,
it's just the dishes are dry and could stand to be re-homed,
or the mail has piled up again on the counter and I can't find
the surface. Perhaps it would be easier to write in a chorus.
I've gone about this all wrong—this is not chess or a set
of stringy marionettes where, if I leave the pieces for a day,
I can return to them unmoved.

A Conversation in Home Depot's Kitchen Department with a Line From *Mrs. Dalloway*

The blush started with a gesture
after poignant questions about bamboo
versus quartz. "What brought you

to town?" The Home Depot kitchen
salesman's eyes widened at three letters,
PhD. He caught my love's eyes and drew

an arch, a rainbow over his belly, over
and over. As if to say, "You know what
to do, forget the countertops, go home,

take her in your bed. Yes, I said your
bed and do what men do." I needed
to shield my own, sought the nearest

turtle shell I could borrow to conceal
my womb the salesman had somehow
conjured in the store before I could tell

him that he wore his narcissism like salt,
that I prefer men to cauliflower, but that he
is inviting me to critically examine

this preference. O how my love stumbled
over how to exit the conversation as he
had once stumbled over the words

crochet and croquet in our early flirtations.
I find solace in a memory: watching
The Andy Griffith Show, how my love knew

the plot—Andy's love interest was a better
shot than him and she waited to show him
publicly at a skeet shooting competition,

"Just wait for her to emasculate him." I thought
perhaps he waited for me to emasculate
the salesman, tell him about the birth

control packet in my purse as a talisman
against the very bodily state the salesman
suggested, the packet he might mistake for Mike and Ikes.

Perhaps my love wanted me to say that he was
the one waiting for me to be ready, that he asked
to be the housewife to let the bacon and bread

walk through the door in my never manicured
fingers, a notion of consistency for the trope
the salesman drew in the middle of the model

kitchens, devoid of domesticity—no flour
left behind after the sponge's bright wipe,
no coffee grounds settled by the machine

like grains of soil after shoveling a fresh grave.
But I laughed, which I felt bounce off
the cabinets—lacking my mother's pink

depression glass or the thrift-store platters
patterned with roses and ribbon—and smack
me. I laughed light, polite. I wish he'd slapped

me, my love, or fucked me in the model kitchen,
asking the salesman pointedly, "Am I doing it right?"

At LongHorn Steakhouse

I can't see how we sit in any romance. Sticky booth, fake
bull horns divert indefinable energy that should course

across a table of lovers or potential lovers or blow the table
to smithereens so we're left with a pile of rubble to make a mess

of ourselves on. I'm in love, but I don't like the frame we're in.
I want to bring it to the local framing shop and pick out

something gaudy and golden. I want our photos black-and-white
for the printer's added pink to our cheeks as though we're fresh

flush off a mattress or off the smithereened table that is still
unrepaired in the LongHorn Steakhouse, where, instead,

they screwed in a plaque above the booth, *Here lay a young couple*
in love, may this destruction be proof of the power of love. But I am

so concerned with showmanship. An orchid on an office desk, a rock
on a ring finger. In this age of audience, I want to find the boxing ring

where my grandparents called each other *Yankee* and *Rebel*
in South Dakota: a crowd screaming for boxers' blood.

Swallowing Blue

We're hooked on a show that tours us
through excessively excessive homes.
One, monstrous and a garish white,
is modeled after yachts with Gucci black

lacquer walls and a gold encrusted
abstraction of a city skyline. Another
has a room for one woman's three
-hundred shoes and two kitchens,

in case she bores of the other. We fell
in love with the house with a maze
and a pavilion yoga studio. We play
the lottery. Watch each week for

the little white globes to bubble over,
wait for the numbers to match ours.
If only we could win. We'd find a plot
of land sandy and fresh, construct

our own with excesses right for us.
Maybe a maze, one kitchen, sea salt
eating at the cushions on the wrap
-around porch so each year I'd have

to find a new affordable set to make
the reedy wicker sittable. I know
he'd like a large house in a small town.
I see the clever game of scale, but I

want a cottage before a big sea. Blue
swallowing the house smaller. His scale
in reverse. How easily we forget our size
as we mill about behind paned windows.

Amendment: how easily we inflate
our size as we pass through archways
proportioned for our heights. How we
sit before the shrunken humans framed

behind the television screen as they stumble
through and by halls and walls built to fit us,
our movements, happiness. The sea cares not.
Swallows snow as if the snow never existed

to fall in the first place, homes who mock
its body from the shore. Sweet swelling, you,
who taunts houses closer, for the moon's
reflection, for the heat that shepherds storms

to doorsteps. I will the danger, to feel small
and swallowed. But you see when I hear
the sea, I sleep. Whereas the sound tells him
to run, run from a hurricane. And as he wakes,

wet and salty, I think, *ah, the sea come in*,
but know the correct answer is sweat.
That the wet cotton pool beneath him
in bed is not the sea coming through

his body but his body ridding himself
of the sea's stress. He tells me of an old
family map. A slice of an island that once
bore his name or a name that is his through

genealogy. He awes at what it would be like
to have this land, with the portion cut out,
reserved for sheep to graze, but not cattle
or horses. To think of only sheep grazing

on grass we own and I want to say we
could have the whole sea before us, no
fences to build and millions of fish nibbling
away at algae deep below and we would not

be able to name them nor mourn them
if they were slaughtered, as the sheep
might be for Frenched lamb. But he thinks
of the wool, and of me and the yarn

I could spin, natural and creamy. How
can I argue at my place in this fantasy
as we run ourselves through the maze,
in our minds, laughing too loud in hopes

we could find each other. How breathless
we are from our sofa, a concoction of love
and dream drawing the air out of our lungs
like pearls plucked from a tired oyster's tongue.

Hope Chest

the chances of a marriage ending in the divorce court... doubled when the bride has no hope chest
—Lane furniture advertisement, 1938

Mother bought me a hope chest
to share the blue house with him.
Mother told me not to tell him
what it was. To reveal the hope
would be to reveal what is not yet
done. To reveal the chest
has already transpired, though she
does not want to know about that
—perhaps for the disorder, or steps
completed out of order. My belongings
a symbol tied up in a trunk—
to use another word, a word I found
and thought no body could be tied
to, and then found in the dictionary.
How wrong I was—for I am
as hopeful as a broken toy, for I find
treasure in the trash, like the crop top
pinned to chain-link like a butterfly
for study, then stored in my hope
chest. This pick is hopeful—hoping
it will fit, hope that the crop top will
cover the chest, the one that has been
revealed, not the one of wood in our
living room that may be a contributing
factor to this union, not yet union,
but union of house and check and chest
and secretly of hope. The old ads advise
it takes years to properly fill a hope
chest, but that summer, settling,
we folded stray quilts and chenille
over the butterfly top. How quickly
the child-sized box filled.

Safe Passing

Let me close up this chaos,
button down the bitter and buckle up,
because morning is about to startle
me. The safe passing of timeless
night, of reality-less dark always
has a blaring, light end. It's called
the sun and as he floods my room
with light, he also blasts my brain
with memories of the day before
(not all good). In this case, not at all
good. As in, fridge-soft spinach
not good, threatening to hop on
a plane not good, as in this blue
house and the kids (we haven't had
but have named) have been keeping
us together all this time. And time
is a trickster, because we were so
bee-busy getting through
time, we forgot to stop and ask
ourselves if love and hate can live
in the same room? And if the answer
is akin to the question of chevron
and houndstooth, my answer
is no. And no is what we kept screaming
with our eyes, shot through with fear,
with change, with dances between
offers of eggs and allergy meds
and silence. There's the possibility
of sacrifice whether it's a chicken
or us on the chopping block, something
will get severed on a rock. It's dizzying
the line between yes and no. It should be clear
as fire and water, day and night and yet
dawn and dusk are hybridous
and we live now on the cusp.

Where We Go From Here

There's no go-to guide like there is for a failed
garden or to lift white water stains from wood.
There's no intuition for this as there is when
turning leftovers into new. It's an autopsy,
working to find out what went wrong, bad:
the blood, the brain, the heart? For a while,
our blood went cold so we held each other
in bed to warm what was left of us, together.
We tried the guide to a failed garden, churned
our soil, sprinkled pellets of fertilizer as trinkets
left with notes for the other to wake up to: A Star
Wars T-shirt, an omelet in the pan. Keep asking
each other, how to move forward and the answer
will surely be nestled like a bullet in one of our guts;
if we dig deep enough we'll extract it with tweezers
as in a game of dark Operation. Our language
has changed. What once coded love, now codes
fraught. We are the weather that humans only
pretend to predict with precision.

All for His

He doesn't go far from bed,
just to work, where he sleep
-talks ice bags and unshelled
shrimp. I about fell out when
he asked me to pass the boiling
pot, check out back to see
the cows are fat and sassy.
I about believed him, but
the drapes shivered in the summer
night and I knew better. I am
to know better, it's my crisis,
perpetually sewing seams back
closed, praising my way
to the shed's cracked foundation,
turned hive for brown mice.
I do so for his dishy face,
buttery and unstressed in sleep,
whose lines I author then,
draw question marks on
his eyelids, thank-yous
behind his ears, dot sugar
crystals on his lips so he
wakes licking a sweet smile
from his face, like a dog's
musty yawn. It's all I can do
to orbit around this bed of ours,
but because it's part of my code,
daughter, sister, daughter,
sister, wife. It's devotion
to learning. He now
never fully cooks my penne
and I am sure to buy pulpless
juice. He silences the hall
candle before joining me for sleep.
Mornings, I blanket him again

as he's kicked them, sheets and all,
to the bed's foot—all for his escape,
not of me or this house, but
whatever it is we all want
to get away from on occasion.
My waltz, my orbit, when
one night, maybe, I'll go out
back and pat those black
and white hides he keeps
singing about in his sleep.

Found

I have almost forgotten he lives here as we open and close like chicory
and moonflowers. Our dog scampers like a tired wind-up toy, but she slows
under the dogwood tree yet to bloom, begins to paw as if restoring life.
And sure enough he strides over through the excited unmown grass, identifies
life too. A small rabbit clinging. She has not done it, of that he is certain, but
what has? He wades into the house to pull from the roll a white trash bag.
I know. So, I turn toward the neighbor's fence, cup my face as if a room all
its own. He tries to twist the bag to leave it airless he tells me, but has to snap
the neck. I heard no snap, the bones so small they didn't even warrant a mark
of passing. Was he sure? He cited the blood spatter against the white bag,
opened the garage's stuttering jaws and settled the tulip-eater beside bags
of orange peels and shrimp tails and used tissues. He came back to the sun-warm
deck, sipped his sweating glass of wine as sweat slicked my thighs.

II.

Our universe
Is only
A colorless onion
You derobe
Sheath by sheath
            Remaining
A disheartening odour
About your nervy hands

—Mina Loy

Fragment

In the lane opposite us, my love and I witness
a car stopped beneath the train trestle, both

driver and passenger depart their vehicle
to remove a Canadian goose from the path

humans take to volley from one side of town
to the other; whether she is hurt or dead is a fact

we cannot discern. We confess to each other
that we've kept objects treasured but broken

—a ceramic lid to a thrift-store dish, a glass
ornament passed down through generations.

This small body plucks our truths. Her long
neck, her night-and-day head, her heathered

torso stay with me each time I pass beneath
the bridge. How different are we? On our way

from point A to point B. The goose bloomed
a fragment in the road for some time, perhaps

other drivers hoped she might animate and fly off,
startled but mobile, just as we harbor our fragments

of glass and pottery waiting for a way to mend,
make whole again. The uncounted number

of shards sequestered in a least-favorite coffee
mug or a tired cardboard box are secrets we want

to ask each other, as we could not ask ourselves
how heavy the goose would feel in our arms.

Hole in the Barn Door Quilt

A hole in the barn door means I'm at it
again. I'm letting in mice, fox kits to sleep
buried in the hay loft. You wouldn't like it,
wanting only to house animals you intend
to keep, who serve your purpose, but I find
such narrow definitions useless for there
is a hole in almost everything useful.
How else did you get in?

The World Is the Goat Who Ate My Dress Clear Off My Body

If gender is a climate
mine's cold, if a landscape,
flat and tidy like rows
of soybeans—that's what
their eyes bat at me, tucked
behind the belt of their offhand
comments: *you're so wifey,* cooed
after a bite into the bundt cake
I baked. The world is the goat
who ate my dress clear off
my body at my second birth
-day party. A second birth,
after which I'd bake spam
mail into my cakes and watch
my cake-eaters fish the shreds
from between their teeth,
listen for the absence of coo.
Silly ole me for letting the lawn
care advertisement slip into the batter
again or the multiplying Capitol
One credit card offers that happened
to get whipped into the cream
cheese icing. *Who? Who?* My mother
would call you an owl to show you
the absent fullness in your sentence,
as she said my fullness would be a weapon
brandished against me, but that I am smarter
than that. A house of cards I'll build
from the secretarial emails
I never should have sent. Not my job.
But neither is the cake, nor the lesson
against the assumption one makes
by something as boxed as a store

-bought cake mix. But how I've got
them in my fields, braving the winds,
petting the goat away from the path
to see the litter of unpicked beans
between the rows they thought
they'd mapped like the backs
of their slap-happy hands.

On Watching *Marie Antoinette* After My Love's Grandfather Died

With the care of our neighbor picking peas freshly ripe
in June for us, you flipped through the cable menu
and settle on her, pink-cheeked Kirsten Dunst in a gown
practically sewn from whipped cream. No cake

or champagne, not even from the goblets you love to cite
as modeled after her breasts. Instead, you munched
on Cheetos Puffs, powdered your fingers orange as she powders
her cheeks pink. Is it her impending death that drew

you to her, the violence of it, contrasted with the slow spread
of your grandfather's? A death that crept up before
you could fly down. The shots of her candy-color shoes
foreshadowed the golf shoes you would find after

the funeral while everyone else pocketed glass paperweights
and Montblanc pens. Nested in the trunk
of your grandfather's Town Car beside the golf bag, they waited
for this storm of ossiferous cancer to pass.

Your grandmother insists you see if your grandfather's crocodile
shoes fit, that she'll mail you them, once she finds them
in this mess. The question I know you will not ask is, *But where
would I wear them?* A question that never left Marie's tongue

as she was fitted for the bodice of each new gown. For now,
you bring home three baseball caps, as ornamental
for you as Marie Antoinette and her silk chapeaux—for her,
these are disposable, for you, irreplaceable. You tell me

you never really knew him, except for the golf balls that rolled
　　　　around his bedroom and the orchid he transplanted
onto the tree in their yard on Date Palm Road. Had Marie
　　　　Antoinette ever tasted a date? In all the lush platters

carried across screen, we spot none. Another Florida summer,
　　　　you call to say we should make fans fashionable again
to cool ourselves in style, a coquettish comment incongruent
　　　　to your context, just as the alcohol poured into your aunt's

glass is of a different note than the champagne poured
　　　　into the glasses of Marie Antoinette's doll-like entourage.
The morning after the service you call to tell me about driving
　　　　the golf cart to sprinkle your grandfather's ashes

over the sand trap he hit most often during his 18 holes,
　　　　how the ashes mounted to less than you imagined
for a burned body. I tell you that what is buried near Marie
　　　　Antoinette's priant may not even be entirely her body.

Like Venus in a Fur Coat

I want a poem that smells like peat
burning in squat, thatch-roofed houses.
A palomino should thunder through
the pillowy smoke at a moment when
it appears she's breaking the gray, biblically

in two. Maybe we could place a king of glass
on the toilet, off in the corner—where we
can't get so close as to resolve the rumor
that he's sewn rods into his clothes to keep
him from cracking. Rewind the poem's

clock to before the queen gained her power
on the chessboard, back when all she
could move was one square diagonally, now
forward. See the difference? Simplicity seems
to be a synonym for grassroots, but pulling up

grass through to its roots, one sees that it's a system
my naked eye can't comprehend. One definition
of naked is *undisguised, blatant* and yes,
there is a blatancy to the body, but that clarity
is cobwebbed by the meaning we put on nudity.

Like Venus in a fur coat, like the curtains
he closes before I lift my shirt over my head.
All this chatter is to say that one person's ideal
is another horse's muck, much like the fur cape
I found slumped on a trash can lid in Toulouse

and that I wore for a year, more out of my pride
in finding such gold, than fashion. But fashion
is another concern, here. Is it not? How peat
and palominos golden, weather fashion heroically
and kings and queens, past their prime, seek

to please like a cherished collection of buttons,
functionless, but nostalgically sweet. Back the tape
up to before we were all expected to arrive
at one agreed upon truth to the point where
poems broke the ground like spring buds
at the sound of a red cardinal's threshing.

Remains

Lovers, were you born on a dining table?
Could your mothers produce enough milk
or did you suckle from the family goat?
Did you suck your thumb or a pair
of fingers? How did you meet the one
you died beside? Or with whom at least now
sleep eternally? In life, did your love snore?
Were they your first kiss? Were you drunk
on wine when you first kissed? Did you argue
over who washed the dishes? Did you use dishes?
Did you enjoy long walks at dusk? Did your love
ever put a flower in your hair, then surprise
you when they kissed your neck? For those
of you who died with your lover, was it a comfort
to not leave this world solo? If you had to choose
one, do you wish you could have one last glass
of water, one more piece of fruit, or one last lick
of your ear before you took your last breath?

Likewise, Here

Little barns, out in the flat, threaten
to melt, like sugar cubes. It is here
I wonder what is inside: crystallized

air or forgotten time, hemmed in
by weathered wood. A horse stands
out front the white barn and turns

the scene to tableau; she begs me
to capture. And it is, likewise, here
I wonder what is inside her: a foal

curled to wait for spring? A coffin
bone turned to plummet toward
hoof? Inside me is fear

for fragility, of wood and body,
of landscape turning to burst
at endeavors to stand fast.

Once Read as Ruin

I.

A torn open fetlock, summer, flies, a red
so real it turns to fiction. Sore, first golf
ball of growth, tears to cleft. I fool myself

into seeing bone, but it's infection—fly
eggs lain in warm wet. A will past my own
body crops through my natural repulse, deals

with the horror of flies dancing in delight
over open meat. This meat I powder pink
to keep dry despite the velvet summer

mud. A candied coating to fragility. Infection
I wrap, fruitless, for as we, humans, pick
at scabs. The liftable lid to our first layer.

Small scale pain. Risk. The horse gnaws
on the bandage I swathed, buries bloodied
gauze in the muck, sure to not let it touch

the sweet alfalfa flake I threw over the fence
into her paddock. What silly pity I hold for
the wound she keeps reopening. How human

an idea to soothe sore with sweet. My child eating
ice cream with a broken leg. My grandmother eating
coffee yogurt after time and space were lost to her.

II.

"St. Ebba the Younger was Abbess of Coldingham, an abbey in the Scottish Borders ... During a Viking raid on Scotland in A.D 879, St. Ebba mutilated her nose and upper lip with a razor, in the hopes of discouraging the invaders from raping her. With her encouragement, the entire community followed suit."

—*Orthodox Saints of the British Isles: Volume III*

as Ebba the Younger

I gathered my flock in the chapter-house.
Chastity, chastity. The men to come,

their wants to take, one sacrifice
for another. Not far from the blood

we take to our lips at the chalice:
what communion in this detachment.

III.
The rain so thick it's a wonder the horse
hadn't swum into the fence post
that now launched from her shoulder

as if a lance, riderless, but ready.
I can't say if it was the sky's
contusion that makes me remember

her this way, but her blood was no
longer red. Purple as the weathered
wood heaving with her labored breath,

as we weighed whether to pull out
the shred of board or if it should stay
as she would lose too much. It's a wonder

she stood, there, on the cross ties,
mud up to her hocks, wet and quiet.
How despite the chill of a summer

storm she didn't dance away
from the hose, but let us spray
down her wait, heat, ache.

IV.

as Ebba the Younger

Chastities I sought to preserve like jams,
canned from orchards tended. From the mouth

of the Tweed to the gates of the abbey, lust
built itself a heavy load, soon jettisoned

by imminent repulsion, in our faces cracked
and bloodied. A new beauty spun in our house

to foil male hunger. Fury, fire, rubble, spurn
turned to ruins, our recipe written for chaotic

conservation, the buried sight of our ruined
faces, molten and won.

V.

"The legend goes: the young Christian Wilgefortis was the daughter of the pagan King of Portugal, who arranged for her to be married to a suitor. The young woman, who had taken a vow of chastity, prayed to be made repulsive and released from the betrothal. Her prayers were answered in the form of a luscious beard. The new facial adornment put off the potential husband, and Wilgefortis's father was so angry that he had her crucified."

—*Saint Wilgefortis: a Bearded Woman with a Queer History*

as the Father

Pretty pawn. I'd sold her hair as health, as possibility
of baby brought forth from between strong legs.

But her prayers of repulsion sang up to Him,
so He sprouted a bane of whiskers on a woman.

How she bristled. How her hair once health now
became monstrosity, other worldly, unweddable,

as she so sought. But how shortly she could carry
such multiplicity, nailed soon a crucifix of contradiction.

VI.
When I dip her muddied, silver tail in the bluing
shampoo, meant for greying ladies to keep shine
in their hair, when I stand at her rump, wait

for the water to turn from suds to grime, she falls
asleep, tired of snaking away from the hose's spritz.
After grazing, when the sun has baked her dry. I braid

her mane along her muscled spine. I do this
grooming to find the day after the tail dusty
again, the braid wild, sprouted with knots and twigs.

VII.
Turned from girl unremarkable to *virgo fortis*, maiden,
unwed girl, or woman that is courageous. *Uncumber,*

Ontkommer one who avoids something, like suffering.
Or anew, *Kümmernis,* grief or anxiety. *Liberata, Librada,*

liberated. *Débarras*, riddance. How many names her beard
sprouted, senses, identities she bore in the hair grown

afresh. With the singly-shod fiddler playing her the tune
of her pious fiction, she hung a lantern, a body self-bridled.

VIII.
In all of this, I have not considered myself.
You see the saints, Ebba and Wilgefortis,
painted as if with the horse in the distance
to illuminate the woman in the foreground.

A horse can denote victory or lust, depending
on tradition. But perhaps there is both victory
and lust in this horse, in these women.
A victory over lust, as when I finish washing

the horse with each ritual of ride and bath,
I take on the horse's grime: a momentary
victory of clean. The dirt, from the ring
kicked up in canter and stride, stains me

an ashen figure, a noseless, bearded girl,
ready to float back to the world invisible.
As I stand at the pump to fill my car with gas,
as I buy a pear for the sugar to balance me

again after these fruitless rites: I am an island
of confusion. *How could this woman show*
herself in such a state. Their eyes scream,
have we no standards any longer, what of taste

decorum, propriety. But the horse tells me
with each post-wash roll in the mud, each tug
at bandage to hide torn open tissue not
to listen. That this exhibition is not new

or futile, but history. Long precedented
in defense of choice. The horse's roll
does not seek to defy me, but stand
as example that she too can choose

her beauty or redefine it with muck and twigs,
blood and scar, as these women chose to preserve
images of themselves through path and presentation
resisted by the men who defined such value

for them no longer. Novel definition
from absence and addition of flesh and hair,
soil and sprig. That the ruin I once read
is not ruin at all, but reinvention.

As unencumbered, as rid of the weight
of expectation, as the horse free from her
halter in a post-rain paddock picks
at the dressing well intended.

III.

In a desperate attempt to know where mother ends and daughter begins, we perform radical surgery.

—Adrienne Rich

Spring Song

We've done it again—left
the windows open so late
into spring that the sugar
ants crawl, in greater
numbers, over the bedsheets.
I can see the encroachment
he feels. Oh how angry
he is that I do not mind,
at times, do not notice.
What if I told him I was ready
to invite the ants to a circle
of song, duck-duck-goose
their little exoskeletoned heads
and pillow fight till we fell, a puddle
of laughter. In this, I take him
outside and show him the four walls
of the unnaturally blue siding
on our saltbox house. Knock
on the artifice that is this space
we have dubbed "home." *I do not*
reject this artifice—I acknowledge
I am complicit, but relish
the violation of ants
crawling up the yellow walls
of our bedroom, singing—
hello, you too are animal.

All the Dear Beasties

A snail can sleep for three years and cows can sleep
standing up, but lie down to dream much like I lie down
restless, wanting everything and sleep. I can hear
the snails slurp back into their shells and cows' great

weight compact the crinkling hay, bedding their night
-cooled stalls. My mother calls this *my mom ears*
growing in, sensitivity to the slightest creaks,
anticipating the patter of feet, my body wants me

to produce, who might seek out a glass of water
or a spot in my bed. But the anticipation is all body,
when my mind only wants sleep. Some dead guy
once said, *after sex, all animals are sad, except roosters*

and women, but I can say I am an exception and often,
not always, find myself sad, feeling I've lost a part like
an earring or a soul. When dogs, domesticated or wild,
hear a yelp, they swarm the source of the wincing cry

to end the suffering, the weakness in the pack.
My father must have wondered whether I was
the weakness in our pack, as I sat for an hour
each night before a nebulizer and cable cartoons;

how the machine-hum helped my thick lungs filter
humid Florida air. My mother became less part
of our pack and more part of the dogs' and, when
needed, their leader. How she tore the Golden

from the Shepherd's jowls over a few kibbles left
behind in a bowl. How she refused to fill the bowl
for days over the Golden's defiance. I tried to get her
to tear me off my brother, as I brushed electric eye

-shadow onto his lids, wanted her to haul me out
to the dog house, firmly exclaim *no*, leave me
there to stew. Maybe, in my fear, a part of me
would split like the tails my brother nearly collected

with each lizard he tried to catch. Everyone would know
my fear, nod to accept the budding regrowth of my finger,
collarbone, or soul. The nub of birth, the grotesqueness
of development, my body so desperately feels I should

engage in, or so my fabled ears signal. How my father
keeps teasing, *six, six children, six babies, six grandchildren,*
but how the repetition gnaws at the joke, how laying
out his own infant christening gown pressed in preservation

plastic solidifies the stray from punch-line. Perhaps I am
part of my mother's pack, the spaniel who caught a land
crab in our yard, ate the body beneath the shell,
and rolled around in what was left, to stink less

of herself, and more like the carcass she'd conquered,
perhaps I'm trying to stink less like myself, less like
the possibility of mother and more anything but. No
more baby powder on my skin, no more baby's breath

in bouquets. I'll plant dogwood and cowslip, lamb's ear
and snail seed. I'll drive to agreed upon gas stations
in response to postings on Craigslist to collect: Zeus,
African soft furred rats, one cat that *must go now*, budgies,

Deuce, Australian Cattle Dog (deaf), brown chickens.
A menagerie of flora and fauna. All my dear beasties
will congregate as if for a sermon, given in Snow
White's soprano. Tails will wag, and tired shells

will still, and hay will crunch under a days' cud chewed.
A shield against the fable or written anew from old tales
of sleep and sex and weakness. And I can say I will be
the exception where my body will not tell me what to do.

Moon Gate

I'm calling to request construction,
an installation in the coming months.
I have a pea in the pod, I've watched
the rabbit die, I'm in the pudding club,
eating for two. I've swallowed
the moon, and soon my lunar body
will no longer obey thresholds,
doorways, vestibules,
however you want to put it.
I want not to feel a rocket
threading a needle's eye, a fat rat
collapsing itself to enter a hole
in weathered brick. Such feats of space
and passage are already penned down
in my fate and, for now, I'd like to feel
a Great White in the sea, a normal-sized me
in a first-class train compartment.

These are my reasons, now for the shape
—a moon gate, with all its wisdom and mythologies
to caress my ballooning frame, for guests not to question
my double body. My body doubled
in size and number. A frame that suits me
now and when my body's achievement can toddle
by my side through the gaping gate
I will tell her of its construction,
how much power she held even before
she'd touch this world. I will call her Helen,
though that will not be her name and she
will never respond to it, but I will know she
moved stones and men before they saw her face.

On My Mother's Recent Heart Attack

I.
Why do we caricature
the heart—mold it to have cartoonish
humps? Fold it to that perfect point: sickening
as puckered lips? Those that
only a child can pull off.

II.
I listen to heartbeats and attend
to the immensity behind
contraction and expansion.

III.
Emotion rattles the body tectonic.

IV.
The first iconography of the heart symbol
was in a 14th-century illustration entitled
Le Roman de la Poire.

V.
I learned the reality of necrotic
tissue as I drove down a highway in a state
I'd never been before and would only stop in
to clear my car of the necrotic tissues
I'd created with disbelief.

VI.
Children cut valentines
by folding red paper in half
and cutting half the symbol
along the seam: those handmade
hearts are more accurate
in their imperfections.

VII.
From the French:
Novel of the Pear.
Novel of the Perry.
Romance of the Round of Beef.
Novel of the Pear Brandy.
Romance of the Perry.
Romance of the Pear Brandy.
Novel of the Round of Beef.
Romance of the Pear.

VIII.
I touch my sternum
to remind myself that I
am a natural rhythm.

IX.
She is painting the walls
of my nursery, on my flight
home. Blue for she was too
stubborn to discover my sex,
or perhaps not caring, out
of the thrill that her body
could carry; those walls
aren't the walls I remember,
but her walls in need of mending.

X.
In the illustration that started this all,
the damsel is on her knees and shares
a pear she peeled with her teeth
with her lover.

XI.
"The heart is a hollow muscular organ that pumps
the blood through the circulatory system by rhythmic
contraction and dilation."

XII.
A family friend called, a former
nurse. I stood in the backyard curbing
tears, not comprehending the trauma of my
mother's heart, her Myocardial Infarction. I endured
the play-by-play of her patho-physiology, fell through the ischemic
cascade. Semilunar valves, my mind left that phone
getting hot on my cheek, left
that summer-dry lawn
and ascended.

XIII.
Love is felt and given long before
romance, felt when skin touches
skin—before we can manipulate
our lips around those three sounds.

XIV.

Language	*Translation of Heart*
Esperanto	Koro
Malay	Hati
Irish	Croí
Swahili	Moyo
Turkish	Kalp
Azerbaijani	ürək
Swedish	Hjärta
Portuguese	Coração
Afrikaans	Hart
Catalan	Cor

XV.
The familiar geometric shape
of the heart is found in much earlier
sources, but instead of depicting the human
organ, they render foliage: fig, ivy,
or even waterlily leaves.

XVI.
Her heart's strength had been quantified.

There's that bit of kitsch: Home
is where the heart is, but I understand
the heart as a home or even a house.

XVII.
Seeing her pink cheeks again
I questioned whether
they were pinker
than last I'd seen.

XVIII.
Other possible origins
for the heart symbol are in the seed
shape of the Silphium plant ancients used as herbal
contraceptive or in the shape of a female's
buttocks, pubic mound, or spread vulva.

XIX.
Chamber: from Old French, chambre,
meaning bedroom.

XX.
The Catholic Church
still contends that the modern
heart came about in the 17th century

when Saint Margaret Mary Alacoque
had a vision of the throbbing
shape surrounded
by thorns.

XXI.
In medieval anatomical descriptions,
the heart was described as a pine cone.

XXII.
S1 corresponds to lub.
S2 corresponds to dub.

I am painfully aware of the relationship
between my blood and my breath—
my mother and myself.

XXIII.
Begun with a girl on her knees,
at a man's feet, exhibiting
her mouth's great abilities.

XXIV.

Language	*Translation of Mother*
Belarusian	маці
Basque	Ama
Triestino	Mare
Czech	Matka
Danish	Mor
Furlan	Mari
Finnish	Äiti
Hindi	Maan
Japanese	Okaasan
Lithuanian	Motina

XXV.
Electricity kindles the blue
LED light. She is charging
a device, in case of another
attack, that would shock her,
spread blue goo over her
chafed chest, would keep her
heart beating; I'm hoping
I don't see blue.

XXVI.
Valve from the Late Middle English, denoting a leaf
of a folding door or halves of a hinged shell.

A normal Left Ventricular Ejection Fraction
ranges from 55-70%.

Blue eyes, blue ocean, blue walls.

Her heart's weakness had been quantified.

XXVII.
Dr. Seuss imagined what would happen
when a heart was, at first, two sizes too
small then grew to be two sizes too big.

XXVIII.
How my heart rate rose
over hearing the state
of my mother's.
The Egyptians believed that the heart
was the source of human wisdom.

XXIX.
Core, the late fourteenth century, from Old French coeur meaning "core of fruit, heart of lettuce" or "human heart," which stems from the Latin *cor* or "heart."

XXX.
The ribcage envelopes the heart
like a minimalist Fabergé egg
around an imperial timepiece.

XXXI.

Language	*Pet Name*	*Translation*
Irish	mo chuisle	my pulse
Greek	ta mátia mou	my little eyes
Swedish	sötnos	sweet nose
Indonesian	buah hatiku	fruit of my heart
Italian	fragolina	little strawberry
Spanish	mi cielito	my little heaven
Dutch	schatje	treasure

XXXII.
This morning I hulled
strawberries and held
that little heart between
my thumb and index
finger, and thought I felt
it pump against the knife
steadied to slice.

XXXIII.
I still wake from deep
sleeps looking, wondering
if she's alive.

Mother

My mother always said sugar
for the shock. Now it's a gin fizz
with a fat lemon pinwheel. Sugar?
Distraction—the sour pucker

gets you through. My mother measures
success by proclaiming she could do it
in high heels—carve a Thanksgiving turkey?
In three-inch stilettos. Climb a ladder
to change a lightbulb? Try it in dictionary
-thick platforms. Knock down a hornet's nest?
Only in t-straps—all the better for fleeing

the angry stings. How to say
you're never the same once
your mother has nearly died. At a rest stop
in Indiana, I collapsed on the sidewalk.
How to say I thought of sugar
and stilettos and a hornet's

nest. How she complained when the hospital
lost her favorite sandals and 30-year-old bra.
How she marveled at how women with big breasts
wear this machine across their chests. The machine
that could save her life again in the night. How she
called the company to suggest designs for future

women with heart conditions and breasts. What power
she holds in the tin of her voice over the phone,
a clam shell of calm—a lemon wheel

of home, but as much as she calls to check on me:
my sleep, my cat with red gums, the warmth
of my house, these calls are for me to hear her,
listen for short breath, for her solution
to her bruising: something about uncrossing

her legs so one leg doesn't weigh down
on the other thigh and leave a purple gulf
she seeks to hide. She tells me she's trained herself

to sit with both high-heeled feet square
on the floor, after returning to work,
far too fast. She never tells me what I know,
that the t-strap heels she wears some days
leave a purple cross across her feet and how

she rubs a minty tincture to erase
the vanity. How to say the curtain
has been torn despite the countless
times I've seen her naked, fresh

from the shower, or mid-clasp of her bra.
She is now more so on the phone, the tired
in her voice tells me so. But the clink

of her glass against her plate during our late
night chat, her late-night dinner, after work,
bruised, tired, breath a bit labored, she tells me
without a word, she'll get through.

Matroneum

Architectonic. Stop. This space
matronly, once, ought not be
reduced vestigial, to a thrust. Let's write,
the Myth of or Mystery at or make
whispers of fairies, ghostly dresses
singing from their once posts, turning
once into ever after. Let's think:

IV.

How many centuries since the first girl—pressing hand against stone—hardly meaning to make an inside—roused you?

—Mary Szybist

The Gift

Some women dream of finding a room
they never knew budded from their house,
beneath a bowing floorboard or behind
the kitchen cupboard. Or plants lifting
their house to the status of tree house, so sky
and ground are no longer a reliable distinction,
but in mine I find a kitten mewing
in unmown grass—coda to when I was a girl
and found a kitten on a walk with my father
and our dog who wanted nothing but to sink
that kitten between his jaws as he did
empty water bottles. My brother and I made

his room a sanctuary, took eye droppers
of whole milk, and dripped little pearls down
the kitten's throat, as our dog threw himself
against the bedroom door. We couldn't keep
the kitten, the quaking frame told us as much.
That night, dryer warmed towels filled
a cardboard box meant for bulk-bought laundry
detergent. The universe brought the little striped
body that needed us, to my cupped palms by luck
and an oddly quiet walk so I could hear his raspy cries
from the sidewalk. I want the gift of another try,
where I get to keep the kitten past one night and, hourly,
return to the cardboard box that smells doubly
of detergent. I'd be a simple equation, but he'd see me
as more, and in that spell, I'd find my place, my room
I never knew grew, a part of me bloomed secretly.

Playing Patience

I.
We didn't have it, sucking air to balloon
our bellies before the mirror. Did so to see
what we'd look like pregnant, before
ever panicking in red panties, but now
patient is all we want to be, for the patience
required in nine months, of nights of no sleep,
produces a panic that turns the red pooled
in our first period sleeps to joy.

II.
We are not made with patience, as we kick
our mothers' distended bellies, asking when
we can get out, as we kick the air from our chairs
when we can't yet feel the time it takes
our mothers to stand over the stove to cook
the rice she forgot goes with dinner.

III.
Scolded *patience, patience, patience.* Only
the repetition begins to sink the sounds
into our bones.

IV.
I watched my mother exercise patience
as my father cleaned the dusty fan blades
an hour before the dinner party.

V.
Patience takes the wet out of your mouth,
the wait leaves you thirsty.

VI.
I learned the patience of waters tested
on a horse who threw me time
and again. Patience, in kicking out
her back legs to unseat me. Patient,
I was, in learning to listen for her
body's whisper. *It's happening again.*

VII.
Life beats us with patience afterward,
with longing for the before of what
we'd been patient for.

VIII.
The body is a vessel consumed
by patience, at first, in fast forward,
as it hurtles toward sex, and then
with working to hamper the growth
of crow's feet or veins spidering
up calves.

IX.
The more we pronounce patience's
plosive p, the more we feel
its quiet mischief.

X.
Patience might divide a human
and a dog, but who
is better for it?

XI.
The root of patience is suffering.

XII.
Two years, my mother hid her
two a.m. walks along the beach,
searching for my stoned brother,
walking alone, night after night.

XIII.
Every night, I get caught in the tide
of my patience, try to measure her
health, take her temperature, brush
her hair, but let her climb a tree
to find flight and fall if she needs.

Mourning Sickness

I live by its insistence
—Sandra McPherson

The washer was filled with light
by which I meant, without
completing my sentence, *with*
light clothes. Our kitchen washed
in light. Here I did not misspeak,
but it is not the kind of light you
may think. Imagine the little sun
of an apricot passed through
a fence and how it might feel
like a dream heard through
a window. This is the light
of which I speak over the sink
and stove, but not with the laundry.
Because the light that we may
all agree is light is too dim
to light anything in this dark.

Woman in White

Before this wall, she hung in an alcove where,
mornings, my mother stood before her vanity
in stockings and underwear dusting color

on her face. In a long white dress that could be her
nightgown, the woman in white wades through grass
-thread holding her basket by its handle. She does not look

through the frame nor at the geese who stay near her
like toddlers. Because of me she stitched this woman,
lying in bed with a fragile, growing belly; because

of me, my mother wove thread through the cotton
as she laid in bed behind the vanity where she'd come
to hang her work. For nine months she stitched

cottages, a girl with her dog, this woman in white
in a field, set her work on the roundness holding me,
keeping thread-wrapped cards around her: a funereal

spray fit for Ophelia, but it was not herself she worried
for but me, having felt too many others pass through
her not yet bodies, but merely thick blood.

At Play

in Burger King's plastic, play place,
adorned with the faint scent
of overdue sanitation. I've pulled
an image of myself from a photograph
for the memory. Pink bike shorts,
patchwork t-shirt, blonde
waterfall ponytail. But he, he is more
ghostly, faceless, of equal height,
hair buzzed close to the skull—
a miniature marine. We must have floundered
together in the ball pit, scrambled up
the alternating over-sized triangles
for stairs, like a salmon ladder in reverse,
to the top of the play place, where we tipped
over and down the slide. But it's at the slide's
mouth where I remember us most.
We face each other our childish, protruding
paunches nearly touching when he asks
without beat, *are you a boy or a girl?* and I want
to pause and exclaim, *of course, what do you think
I am, a horse? A Venus fly trap? I'm a girl, silly,
in my ponytail and pink shorts,* or something
to that effect, but then I give the simplest
answer, the questions to clear confusion,
or what I then thought would help us
continue our runs and squeals over bacteria
-laden plastic. But if I could return to that self,
back to that Burger King before they wrecked
the play place flat, I'd spend more time
at the slide's mouth as kids slid between
our almost-united bellies and we'd
discuss, boy and girl, boy and girl:
why he questioned, why I answered,
how my answer changed us and our play.
Maybe we'd pull together metal

and vinyl chairs for me to lie down on
and he'd sit at the entrance to the ball pit,
legs crossed, not answer any of *my* questions,
but listen, and I might say how this is good
practice for him and he would grunt
in acknowledgement as he is bred to do
and I would want more as I am bred to want,
but soon we'd kick the chairs over, lace hands
and return to children, licking our fry-oily fingers,
and flounder further into the play place.

Your Childhood Is Showing

I watch him watch
snow fall for the first time
through my windshield.
He cranes his neck to find the source
of wet cotton's fall, no, tasteless summer
snow cones' glop down to melt
on my engine-warm car. His eyes glint;
I decide his childhood is skipping out
from the space between his socket
and eye. Mine escapes
from my mouth's corner, in the high
pitched voice I use to say, *Dad.*
Though I hate it, I can't help myself
when he calls. His childhood escapes
in awe as mine untwines
as a habit to hold on.

Let Me In

To survive a fire, logic says,
wait by water. A lake,
pond, or reservoir. The trick,
if and when the fire arrives, is to sink
deep enough so the water can hush
the flames. The fool believes
she's safe in water, no matter,
but truth is water
can burn. If the fire is hot
enough, water can burn so even
with the smoke swelling,
practice, now, holding your breath.
Deep inhale. Feel your lungs tap
your diaphragm. A bit like a choral bell
ringer. A bit like a fist at the door. *Let me in.*
Let me in. The air cries. Then smack
your lips together while your nostrils flare
wishing they could cheat, cheat,
but don't. Remember you will be submerged.
Go in the bath. Yes, right now. Lie back,
as you did as a child, trying to scare
your parents something fierce. Lead them
to believe their turn for the dryer-warm
towel was the difference.
Practice for the water,
but, in the end, don't beat yourself,
if you can't hold on.

V.

There is always within her at least a little of that good mother's milk. She writes in white ink.

— Hélène Cixous

Stormsleep

Momma wouldn't let us all fall
asleep in storms. Fear of water's
rise, of us sleeping

to death meant she didn't sleep
so we could. Some nights,
storms had nothing

to do with the weather. Momma
didn't sleep in those either. We knew
the next morning.

Eyes grayer than her gray-
blue, cloudy from traveling
the house all night.

Small-Scale Altimetry

He talks of the topography of my body, its altitudes; his fingers
practice this small-scale altimetry. We are no longer at sea
level—near zero where we each grew up, where we, fall
and summer, stacked sandbags for coming storms,
for the water that swept under and into our house
whose strength would carry us further inland
were it not for the neighboring houses
or so I dreamed.

Today, there is rain outside our Midwestern salt box
-blue house, a drizzle, really. We laugh at going out
to plant strawberries bought after the success
of the front yard's tulips. We don't know
how many feet above the sea we sit
now, don't care, but digging
for these roots I miss

digging in my childhood backyard, hitting brimming water
from the sea, miss the salty mud, velvet in my hands.
This *we* is not the *we* of my childhood, but the *we*
of my now, the he who has touched me
in the yard where I dug to the sea,
but never saw me unearth
the ocean, but now watches
my topography,

a topography unlike that of our childhood home, bend
to work this new earth, rich and rain-damp, to quarry
a new topography for strawberries in our backyard
so that we can bring the jeweled drops inside,
slice them open, and freckle sugar over
their halves. It will be summer
when we pick them.
Wet and soil

-mired we'll strip in the shower, reveal the clean skin
beneath our clothes, let the water pour over
our rain-chilled bodies. He, standing there
before me beneath the hot shower
head, will kneel before me
with soap in his hand,
begin to wash
my feet first.

Water Song

Rain blinks a code
I should know, waxes
into a wound spiced
numb with listening.
All the little words curl
in like hounds done
barking, like leaves
piled for burning,
crumbs to make clean
a table. I am to sew
my teeth, soft
and kissable, but I don't
listen. I'd rather
bleed forever, sign
my life away with
a needle, sewn shut
without possibility
for undoing, lie back
in animal-warm straw,
taken by pleasure's
eddies. There might be
a constellation of votives
to encircle me briefly,
to stave the hunger,
thunder, waxing I am
expected to thunder
through, but water
does not obey as land,
and the votives stray,
pouting irregular circles,
a current currently in
change. The water carries
on and I have no choice
but to listen, consent
to its direction and song.

The Call

Sundays I hear church bells through
my kitchen window. Tuesdays it's sirens.
Take a tuning fork to my porcelain
sink, re-sing the note for you. Most nights
I hear my name. Call to tell you, to ask,
but you say it must have been the wind.
Each time I call I drop a whole herring
down my throat, harbor salt in my jaws'
hinges, working to equate you with salt
or, better yet, summer lightning.

In April

She must have carried
her belly around like a fish
bowl. Careful not to knock into corners,
bash the little gold body floating inside her.
Despite her care, it took her seven tries to carry
one home. Seven times she saw it float, belly up
in the bowl. Wanting to smash bowl, body,
the blow dryer on its hook. How her body
must have felt like snow
in this April.

On Driving to Find Him at Midnight When All He Could Do Was Turn Left

I miss when things were mythical,
he slumps on the fault
-line between driveway and winter
-dry brush. *I just want you,*
he sheds his coat
like snake skin. He lies
a chalked corpse, wishing
some star'd suck him up
through a straw—he'd forget
his body. He leaves
his coat clear on the driveway.
His clothes puddle ocean
-dark on the bathroom floor,
his voice climbs higher
in tiled echo. *Don't you appreciate*
how I orchestrate everything
for you? I wow how
even in this state he thinks himself
a mini-god. I ask him countless
to sleep. *I'll walk out that door*
straight into traffic.
I want to point out
our street at, now,
2am isn't exactly a bustling thoroughfare.
That he'd have better luck at 3pm
on a school day when the multi-laned
lines of minivans fill our neighborhood
street like a properly stuffed
sausage. *You're naked,*
it's 30 degrees, you'd freeze
before finding someone to hit you
at this hour.

Fish Wife

It's mostly a life
of waiting and counting.
Each night I unhook
the stars, restrike them the next,
all floated matches red
before ignition. Scales the only
glitter tumbling onto my lap.
To hear beauty, I fashion
earrings from his tired hooks
and bait, brightest in my shiplap
shack. He's well salted from years
of ocean spit and slap. But it all
falls away when honeyed tea hits
his belly, when he calls me
kitten, slips his hand to the soft
of my thigh. It's a ritual
of bringing him back
to land. I've taught myself
all the right knots that lasso
his waist back to his chair,
our bed, my table.
I am a denounced planet
he burns for. It sounds
bad, but it's balance.
Not so key that the winds listen
for my footfall, but not so forgotten
that they sweep me up and out
like the nests of fur I brush
out the door.

Widow's Walk

I walk my widow's walk not to look
out on the sea and expect him
to climb from the surf ragged
and torn, all effort to return to me,
but so I can announce my spidery
existence as I web my way through
my paces as to how to proceed.
Each evening I climb with a light
and to my neighbors I must look
like hope. A small woman-made light
-house directing one phantom ship,
but the light is for me to watch my hands
age each night, for the veins that spider
their way up from my palms' depths,
to watch how night floats through
sleep that escapes me, to watch how
empty this house is without him.
But empty is a treacherous word—
often a placeholder for grief,
for the missing, subtraction, but what
if I see this word as addition. For the space
I've gained in the wardrobe, for the far
fewer dishes left in the sink, for the bed
I can starfish my way through sleep
when I find it and not feel guilty for finding
him on the floor. And what if he sees
his subtraction as gain, for he has left
behind the pressures of closing the house's
shutters for storms, of holding my hand
when we walk into town. What if he lies
on another beach somewhere? What if he
knows that all he owns is his body
and that the sand is not his, but has no desire
to make it so and the palm trees are not his
and yet they drop coconuts for him. This is not

far from how the rain falls for me and I open
my mouth knowing no one will turn the corner
and interrupt my joy.

Curling to a New Sky

The whey of winter sleeps
restlessly trying to take
with it sweating windows
and vents whose lungs tire
of heaving hot air. Tulips
unwreathe through winter
-worn dirt like young women
unbraiding their hair after sleep,
curling to the new day's sky,
but old webs have yet to release
dawn's unfrozen dew and the morning
tea is still hot and the night-rum
still dark for it snowed early
this morning and the curb's wildflowers
shivered closed—naked girls
wrapping themselves in towels. Morning's rise
is still slow from the quilts
that weighed us down through the cold
dawn. Bare arms blink at the sun before slipping
back into their knits when wind
outweighs the warmth. But we keep
trying to entice spring with our bodies,
daring to sport a thin sock, to brave
the door, hatless, at first, daring to defy
what the sky tells us,
instead telling ourselves that we can
will the sky to give.

Acknowledgements

45th Parallel	"On Watching *Marie Antoinette* After My Love's Grandfather Died"
Atticus Review	"The World Is the Goat Who Ate My Dress Clear Off My Body"
Barnstorm Journal	"Fragment"
Cathexis Northwest	"All for His"
	"Moon Gate"
Harpur Palate	"A Conversation in Home Depot's Kitchen Department with a Line From *Mrs. Dalloway*"
jubilat	"The Call"
Kettle Blue Review	"In April"
Lost Pilots	"Like a Salmon (or Fool in a Blue House)"
Meridian	"Hole in the Barn Door Quilt"
Rabbit Catastrophe	"Once Read as Ruin"
Rumble Fish Quarterly	"Woman in White"
Storyscape Journal	"Matroneum"
Tampa Review	"Fish Wife"
	"Hole in the Barn Door Quilt"
	"Like a Salmon (or Fool in a Blue House)"
	"Remains"
	"Small-Scale Altimetry"
	"The World Is the Goat Who Ate My Dress Clear Off My Body"
That Literary Magazine	"Where We Go From Here"
Variant Lit	"Likewise, Here"

The following poems appeared in *Once Read as Ruin,* a finalist for Finishing Line Press' New Women's Voices Chapbook Prize: "At Longhorn Steakhouse," "Fish Wife," "Found," "In April," "Hole in the Barn Door Quilt," "Matroneum," "Once Read as Ruin," "Swallowing Blue," "The Call," "Water Song," and "Widow's Walk" (then titled "A Small Woman-Made Lighthouse").

"A Conversation in Home Depot's Kitchen Department with a Line From *Mrs. Dalloway*" won the 2022 Milton Kessler Poetry Prize from *Harpur Palate.*

"Like a Salmon (or Fool in a Blue House)" was selected for the 2022 *Best New Poets* anthology.

An abundance of gratitude to: Nicholas Molbert, Jessica Tanck, Aumaine Rose Smith, Janice Harrington, Corey Van Landingham, Christopher Kempf, Benjamin Miller, Maldonado-Velez, Skyler Lalone, Taylor Micks, Annah Sidigu, and Alexandra Tanner. Much gratitude to the University of Tampa Press for bringing this book into the world. With deep affection, a special thanks to William Logan, Michael Hofmann, Dr. Michael Bassett, and Michael Madonick. And, of course, all my love to my loving and supportive family, and friends, mentors, and more dear ones who may not be listed here.

About the Author

Katherine Gaffney completed her MFA at the University of Illinois at Urbana-Champaign and is currently working on her PhD at the University of Southern Mississippi. Her work has previously appeared in *Mississippi Review*, *Bellevue Literary Review*, *Frontier Poetry*, *Penn Review*, *Smartish Pace*, *Permafrost*, and elsewhere. She has attended the Tin House Summer Writing Workshop, the SAFTA Residency, and the Sewanee Writers' Conference as a scholar. Her first chapbook, *Once Read as Ruin*, was published by Finishing Line Press. *Fool in a Blue House* is her first full-length collection.

About the Book

Fool in a Blue House is set in Garamond Premier Pro digital fonts, based on original metal types by Claude Garamond and Robert Granjon that were designed and cast in Paris, France, in the sixteenth century. The book was designed and typeset by Wesley Kapp at the University of Tampa Press.

Printed in Great Britain
by Amazon